Journey of a Lifetime

The Jewish Life Cycle Book

Behrman House

Dedicated with love and thanks to my husband,

Michael Klayman, for his constant support and wisdom,

and extraordinary skills as an educator;

And with gratitude to my editors, Adam Bengal, Adam Siegel,

and Ruby Strauss, for their insight and guidance.

The author and publisher gratefully acknowledge the following sources of photographs for this book:
Bill Aron: 9, 20, 64, 67, 75; Creative Image: 33, 35, 38, 43, 45, 49, 55, 76, 83, 87, 88; Rameshwar
Das/Monkmeyer: 61; Roger Dollarhide/Monkmeyer: 13, 63; Hershkowitz/Monkmeyer: 71, 73; David
Hollander and Congregation B'nai Jeshurun of Short Hills, New Jersey: 53; Francene Keery: 31.

Musleah, Rahel
Journey of a lifetime : the Jewish life cycle book / Rahel Musleah
        p. cm.
    ISBN 0-87441-631-0
    1. Judaism—Customs and practices—Juvenile literature. 2. Life cycle,
Human—Religious aspects—Judaism—Juvenile literature. 3. Judaism—Liturgy—
Juvenile literature. 4. Jewish religious education—Textbooks for children. I. Title.
                                                97-1396
                                                CIP

Book Design: Howard Levy Design
Project Editors: Adam Siegel, Ruby Strauss
Illustrated by Allan Eitzen (pages 23, 36-37, 57, 69, 78-79) and Larry Nolte

Published by Behrman House, Inc.
235 Watchung Avenue
West Orange, NJ 07052

MANUFACTURED IN THE UNITED STATES OF AMERICA

Contents

Introduction
The Journey Begins

••

Imagine that you are setting out on a long journey—the experience of a lifetime. Your trip will be filled with adventure and celebration. There will be ordinary days along the way, and even some sad moments. But these will help you reach special places you will remember all your life.

Growing up to be a Jewish adult is this kind of journey. From the moment you are born, special celebrations help mark the milestones along the way: receiving a Hebrew name, beginning religious school, becoming a Bat Mitzvah or Bar Mitzvah, reaching Confirmation, and getting married. These events are all occasions for celebration.

Why is the Jewish part of this journey important? We all receive a name when we are born. But if you're Jewish, receiving a name means more than filling out a birth certificate. It means celebrating the event with a ceremony that connects you to Jewish people around the world and throughout history. Everyone turns thirteen. But when you're Jewish, that means more than a birthday cake with thirteen candles to blow out. It means becoming a Bat or Bar Mitzvah—celebrating the beginning of Jewish adulthood. Adding the "Jewish" part to the journey makes the ordinary unforgettable.

This book will help prepare you for the adventure of growing up Jewishly. It's like a guide or a road map that points out places of interest to visit, suggests side trips you won't want to miss, and even includes signs and symbols that give meaning and direction to your travels. Get ready to embark on the journey of a lifetime.

Nesiah tovah! Have a wonderful journey!

1

Brit Milah
Brit Bat

Welcoming a Baby

Do you remember the last time you made an agreement with someone? Maybe you promised to teach your sister how to rollerblade if she would take out the trash. Perhaps you promised to clean your room once a week if your parents would drive you to soccer practice. How did you remember to keep your part of the agreement?

The Torah tells us about a series of agreements, or covenants, our ancestors made with God. In Hebrew, a covenant is called a *brit*. The first *brit* was between God and Noah. In this agreement, God promised never again to destroy the earth, and in return, God asked Noah and his descendants to strive to be good and to fill the world with people. The second *brit* was made between God and our biblical ancestor Abraham. God promised to make Abraham the father of great nations and Abraham promised that he and all his children and his children's children would follow God's teachings. The great Covenant was made at Mount Sinai between God and all the Children of Israel after God freed them from slavery in Egypt. In this *brit*, the Israelites promised to follow God's laws and teachings, which are called mitzvot. In return, God promised to make the Jewish people a great nation. God made this Covenant not only with the Israelites who stood at Mount Sinai thousands of years ago, but also with their children and their children's children. And from generation to generation, we continue to keep our part of this agreement.

Brit Milah

Different ceremonies bring Jewish baby boys and baby girls into the Covenant with God.

Baby boys enter the Covenant the way Abraham did more than four thousand years ago. The Torah tells us that God commanded Abraham to circumcise himself and his son as a symbol of the covenant Abraham had entered into with God.

The Hebrew word *milah* means "circumcision." The circumcision ceremony is therefore called a Brit Milah, which means "Covenant of the Circumcision."

Brit Milah is a physical reminder of our Covenant with God. Jews everywhere, in all times and places, are bound to God as one people through this mitzvah.

Do you remember the story of Noah and the ark? After the Flood, God made a promise to Noah. God promised never again to destroy the world.
Do you remember the symbol of God's promise? How do you remember to keep promises you have made?

Words to Remember

BRIT
Covenant

MILAH
Circumcision—the cutting off of the foreskin from the end of the penis

MITZVAH (MITZVOT)
God's commandment(s)

The Brit Milah Ceremony

No matter what part of the world you live in, the ceremony for a Brit Milah is almost always the same. Here is what happens during the ceremony:

1. The baby's godparents carry the baby into the room where the circumcision will take place. (The godparents will help teach the baby how to live a Jewish life as he grows up.)

2. Family and friends say, "Welcome! Blessed is he who is about to enter the Covenant."

3. The godparents give the baby to the *mohel*, the person who performs the circumcision.

4. The *sandek* holds the baby during the circumcision. (It is a great honor to be a *sandek*.)

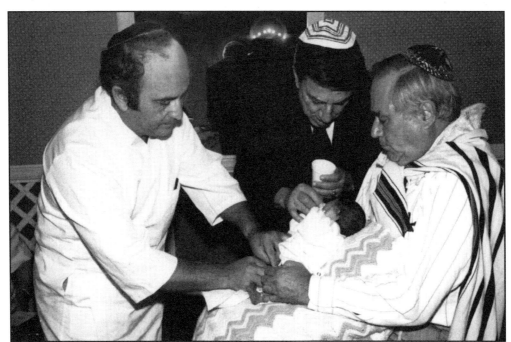

5. The *mohel* performs the circumcision, which takes only a few seconds and is almost painless. Then the *mohel* recites the Kiddush, the blessing over the wine, announces the baby's Hebrew and English names, and recites other blessings and prayers.

6. Family and friends enjoy a *seudat mitzvah*, a festive meal prepared to celebrate the performance of a mitzvah.

Words to Remember

MOHEL
A person who performs a circumcision

SANDEK
The person who holds the baby during a circumcision

SEUDAT MITZVAH
A joyous meal served after the performance of a mitzvah

The velvet cover hanging over the back of this chair is embroidered with silk thread to form Hebrew words. These include the name of the prophet who is invited to every Brit Milah ceremony. Can you find the Hebrew letters that spell Eliyahu Ha-navi? What is this prophet's English name?

A Special Guest

Family and friends come to the Brit Milah ceremony to help welcome the baby into the Jewish people's Covenant with God. Parents, grandparents, aunts, uncles, and cousins—all share in the performance of the mitzvah of Brit Milah as a new member joins the Jewish community.

The guest list for a Brit Milah always includes one special person—the prophet Elijah. According to legend, Elijah doubted that the Jews would continue to honor their *brit* with God. To show Elijah that he was wrong, God instructed that the prophet be present at every circumcision. And so we set aside a special chair for Elijah at every Brit Milah. In this way, Elijah can witness our people's ongoing commitment to raising Jewish children.

To what other celebration is Elijah invited? How do we welcome him during that holiday?

It's a Mitzvah!

Did you know that it's a mitzvah to have one's son circumcised? In the Torah, it is written: "At the age of eight days, every male among you throughout the generations shall be circumcised."

GENESIS
17:12

Brit Bat

Some Jewish life-cycle rituals, like Brit Milah, are very old. They have been performed for thousands of years. Other life-cycle rituals are much newer. One example is Brit Bat, which means "Covenant of the Daughter." Brit Bat is also called Simḥat Bat, which means "Rejoicing over a Daughter." This ceremony brings a Jewish baby girl into the Covenant with God. Parents can choose different ways to bring their daughter into the Covenant.

Some families mark the birth of a daughter by reading from the Torah in the synagogue on the Shabbat after she is born. A special prayer for the baby is recited, and her Hebrew and English names are announced to the congregation.

Other families are called to the *bimah*, the platform in front of the Holy Ark, on a Friday evening soon after the birth of the baby. A formal naming ceremony takes place, after which the rabbi recites the same traditional blessing that is recited at a Brit Milah.

Some families have created a home celebration that is similar to a Brit Milah. The baby is named and blessed during the ceremony. The parents may light candles in honor of their daughter and recite verses from the Bible that contain her Hebrew name. Or the parents may wrap the baby in a *tallit*, a prayer shawl, to symbolize God's warm, comforting presence. As at a Brit Milah, the guests enjoy a *seudat mitzvah* to celebrate the performance of a mitzvah.

Something to Talk About

Jews have always performed ceremonies that help bring the Jewish community closer to God. Brit Bat is an example of a new ritual that continues to change as people add new customs to it. *What important events in your life would you like to celebrate in a Jewish way?*

Redeeming the Firstborn

The birth of every Jewish baby girl and boy is a time for celebration. It is a time to welcome the child into the Jewish community by performing either a Brit Bat or a Brit Milah. Either one of these rituals is performed only once in each person's life. There is another ceremony that is performed only once in a *family's* life. It is an ancient ceremony called Pidyon Ha-Ben, which means "Redeeming the Son."

In the Bible, God commanded that each firstborn son devote his life to God's service by working for the priests in the Holy Temple. But God also commanded that firstborn sons may be released from this obligation through a payment of money. To fulfill this mitzvah, a special ceremony was created.

It is like a play. Here's the script: The parents hand the baby to a *kohen*, a descendant of the priests who conducted sacrifices and worship services in the ancient Temple.

Kohen: What would you prefer? To give this child to me and have me dedicate him to serve God, or to redeem him as demanded by the Torah?

IT'S A FACT!

Pidyon Ha-Ben is performed when the firstborn son is thirty-one days old.

It's a Mitzvah!

Pidyon Ha-Ben is a mitzvah. In the Torah, God instructed Aaron: "You will redeem the firstborn.... You shall redeem him at the age of one month for the price of five shekels."

NUMBERS 18:15-16

Parent: I wish to redeem my son, and here is the fee.

Kohen: I accept the money as a substitute for this child.
(Kohen holds coins over baby's head.)

Long ago, parents paid five shekels (ancient Hebrew coins) to redeem their son. Today many parents use five silver dollars instead. The money is later donated to tzedakah.

Some families feel that there should also be a redemption ceremony when the first child is a girl. Therefore, a Pidyon Ha-Bat ("Redeeming the Daughter") ceremony may be performed for a firstborn daughter. It follows the same pattern as a Pidyon Ha-Ben ceremony.

Words to Remember

BRIT MILAH
Covenant of the Circumcision

BRIT BAT
Covenant of the Daughter

SIMHAT BAT
Rejoicing over a Daughter

PIDYON HA-BEN
Redeeming the Son

PIDYON HA-BAT
Redeeming the Daughter

MAKE A BRIT

The Brit Milah and Brit Bat ceremonies celebrate the agreement between God and the Jewish people. Through these rituals, babies are brought into our Covenant with God.

In everyday life, we make agreements all the time. We make them with sisters and brothers, parents and friends.

Describe three agreements you have made with family members or friends.

1. _____

2. _____

3. _____

Did you keep the agreements? Was it difficult to keep them? Explain.

_____

Now list three things you are required to do because you have entered into the Jewish people's Covenant with God. For example, you hear the shofar sounded on Rosh Hashanah. You help build a sukkah. What else are you commanded to do?

1. _____

2. _____

3. _____

Be a Fund-Raiser!

The birth of a baby is a joyous time. We are thankful for a new life and for a new member of the Jewish people. This is a time when many people give tzedakah to share their happiness with those who need help.

Organized charity campaigns, such as the United Jewish Appeal, the United Way, and the American Cancer Society use slogans to help persuade people to donate money to their causes. Here are some examples: "We are one." "Give life and hope." "The gift that never stops giving."

Create a slogan for a billboard. Your slogan should urge families who have just had a new baby to give tzedakah.

2 Baby Naming

Receiving a Hebrew Name

Have you ever gone to camp? Did your parents write your name with markers, or sew name tags on your socks, shirts, and swimsuits? Everyone's camp clothes look pretty much alike, and if they are not labeled, campers can't tell which are theirs.

But a person's name is much more than a label to be sewn on clothes. It identifies the person. And your name identifies a special person who is different from all others—you!

When parents see their newborn baby, they wonder what the future will hold for their child. They might wonder, "Will she grow to be athletic and kind like Aunt Rachel? Will he become musical and helpful like Grandpa Max?" Your parents chose your name with care. You might have been named after a person your parents loved, or perhaps you were named for someone in the Bible. Your name may mean "beautiful flower" or "mighty tree." Whatever it is, your name reflects the hopes and dreams that your parents have for you.

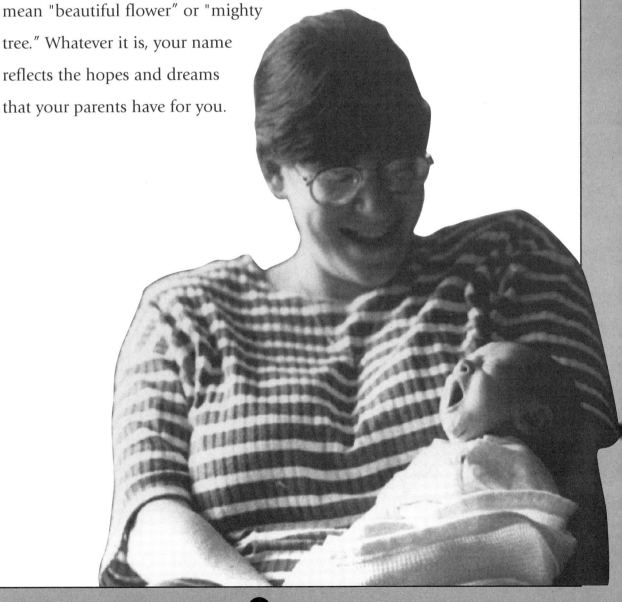

Hebrew Names

Every Jewish baby is given a Hebrew name. Our Hebrew names link us to the Jewish people.

Most Jews live in countries where Hebrew is not the official language. So they often have two first names. For example, you may have an English name as well as a Hebrew one. If so, you probably use your English name in your everyday life, but you use your Hebrew name at all the important moments in your Jewish life. You will be called to the Torah by your Hebrew name

Some Jews believe that certain qualities—such as intelligence, humor, and thoughtfulness—can come with a name. When Jewish parents name their child after someone, they hope the child will have that person's same qualities. *Did your parents name you after someone? If so, who?*

when you become a Bat Mitzvah or a Bar Mitzvah. When you get married, your Hebrew name will be written on your marriage certificate.

Everyday names are officially given when parents sign their child's birth certificate. Hebrew names, however, are given at a religious ceremony. Boys receive their Hebrew names at the Brit Milah ceremony. Girls receive theirs at the Brit Bat ceremony.

Words to Remember

BAT
Daughter of

BEN
Son of

SURNAME
Last name or family name

What Hebrew Names Look Like

Hebrew names have a special form. We say the first name. Then we say *ben* for a boy, which is Hebrew for "son of." For a girl, we say *bat*, which is Hebrew for "daughter of." *Ben* or *bat* is followed by our parents' Hebrew names. Jews have used names like these for thousands of years.

Practice writing your full Hebrew name:

For a Girl

_____ *bat* _____ *v′* _____

(my Hebrew name) daughter of *(my father's Hebrew name)* and *(my mother's Hebrew name)*

For a Boy

_____ *ben* _____ *v′* _____

(my Hebrew name) son of *(my father's Hebrew name)* and *(my mother's Hebrew name)*

Choosing a Hebrew Name

Parents choose a Hebrew name for their son or daughter in different ways. Many parents choose their child's Hebrew name from people in the Bible. Naming children after our ancestors—such as Joshua, Rachel, Jacob, and Sarah—is a way of honoring both our history and the new baby.

Some Hebrew names come from Hebrew words. They are often words from nature, such as Ilana ("tree"), Arieh ("lion"), or Devorah ("bee").

Jewish families from Eastern Europe often name a child after a relative only after the relative has died. Jewish families from Spain, Italy, North Africa, and the Middle East often name a child after a living relative.

The family of the famous Rabbi Hillel repeated the same four names for boys—Hillel, Simon, Gamliel, and Judah—for five hundred years. The men who originally had those names must have been dearly loved and greatly respected by the members of that family.
Is there a name that is popular in your family?

In many Jewish families, one or a few names are used again and again. They may be seen as an inheritance that is passed from generation to generation. Or they may be seen as a chain that links the generations.

Suppose you are a girl whose great-great-grandmother's name was Sarah. Your grandmother was named after her, and you were named after your grandmother. Your name, Sarah, connects you to your great-great-grandmother.

From the Bible

GENESIS 18 and 21

Read this text to find out how our biblical ancestor Isaac got his name.

*A*braham and Sarah were growing very old, and they had no children. Then God came to Abraham and told him, "I will give you and Sarah a son."

When Abraham heard God's words, he thought to himself, "Sarah and I are too old to have a child. Can God's words be true?" Sarah, standing in the doorway of their tent, also doubted God's words. Sarah laughed at the idea of having a child in her old age.

Now God knew what Abraham was thinking. And God said, "Think what you like. You and Sarah shall have a son."

And God remembered Sarah. She had a son, just as God had promised. And Abraham named him Yitzḥak (Isaac), which means "child of laughter."

Sarah said, "God brought me laughter. Everyone who hears how I had a son in my old age will be happy with me."

Family Names

Jews did not always have last names, or surnames. Family names were not necessary when Jews lived in small villages and had little contact with the outside world. Someone could simply be called Chaim ben Avraham (Chaim the son of Abraham). It was only about two hundred years ago that European countries began to require all people to take surnames. So your last name is probably not very old at all.

Something to  About

The first man, Adam, was named for the earth, which in Hebrew is adamah. Why was this a suitable name for Adam? What does your Hebrew name mean? Ask your parents how they chose your name. In what way is your name like you? Explain.

Names as Gifts

Pirke Avot, the Ethics of the Fathers, teaches that there are three crowns: the crown of the priesthood, the crown of Torah, and the crown of kingship. But the crown of a good name is better than them all. You can make your name a "good name," a *shem tov* in Hebrew, by behaving righteously, by following God's commandments.

The names we have are gifts from our parents, gifts that remain with us throughout our lives. Our names can remind us of the special things that our parents wished for us when we were born and the love they felt when they chose them.

Our names also connect us to family members. And they connect us to our people. It is our responsibility to wear our names with pride and to remember that "the crown of a good name" is the most beautiful crown of all!

WHAT DO YOU THINK?

Pirke Avot teaches that the crown of a good name means more than the crown worn by a king or a queen. Why? What can you do to earn a good name, a **shem tov**?

My Name

You may have been given the name of someone in your family, someone famous in history, or someone famous today. Or you may have been given a name because your parents like the sound of it or admire what it stands for.

My English first name: _____

My English middle name: _____

My Hebrew first name: _____

My Hebrew middle name: _____

Find out as much as you can about your Hebrew name. If you were named for a person, tell what he or she looked or looks like. Tell about his or her personality. Write a story about the person you are named for.

If your name is Hebrew for something that can be described (as a tree can be), tell what the thing looks like. If your name is Hebrew for an idea (like strength), tell what the idea means. If your name comes from the Bible, retell a story about that biblical character.

_____

_____

_____

_____

Complete the Sentences

Crown   Nature   Ben

Earth   Bat   Torah

Use the words in the box above to complete the sentences.

1. Adam, the first man, was named for the Hebrew word for _____.

2. The Hebrew word for "son of" is _____.

3. We use our Hebrew names when we are called to the _____.

4. The Hebrew word for "daughter of" is _____.

5. Many Hebrew names come from things in _____.

6. A good name is like a _____.

THE CROWN OF A GOOD NAME

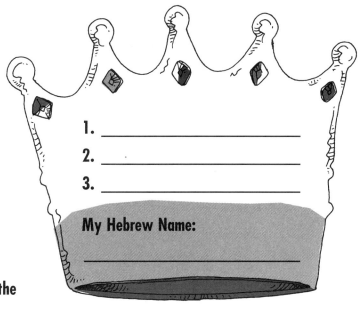

1. _____
2. _____
3. _____

My Hebrew Name:

_____

Write your Hebrew name on the rim of the crown. Inside the crown, list three things you have done to give yourself a *shem tov*.

What's in a Name?

Use the name dictionary on the next page to answer the following questions.

1. In Eastern Europe every town had at least one baker, so baking was a common occupation. Write two Jewish family names that mean "baker." _____

2. In order to be kosher, meat must be prepared in a special way. Every town where Jews lived needed a kosher butcher. Write two names that mean "butcher." _____

3. Many Jews in Eastern Europe made and sold jewelry. Write two Jewish family names from the list that mean "jewelers."

   _____

4. If you had lived in a village in Eastern Europe, to whom would you probably have gone:

   for a haircut? To Mr. _____

   to buy bread? to Mrs. _____

   to get medicine? to Mr. _____

   to buy fish? to Mrs. _____

A DICTIONARY of Jewish Family Names

Many Jewish family names come from the jobs our ancestors had in Eastern Europe many years ago. Is your family name on this list?

Abzug: printer
Ackerman: plowman
Balsam: pharmacist
Beckman: baker
Besser: tax collector
Binder: bookbinder
Blecher: tinsmith
Bodner: barrel maker
Broitman: baker
Bronfman: whiskey merchant
Buxbaum: woodworker
Chait: tailor
Chasin: cantor
Citron: lemon seller
Dauber: pigeon seller
Drucker: printer
Einstein: mason
Feinberg: wine merchant
Feinstein: jeweler
Flaxman: flax dealer
Fleishman: butcher
Forman: teamster
Futterman: furrier
Garber: tanner

Garfunkel: diamond merchant
Gittelman: cap maker
Glass: glassmaker
Goldstein: goldsmith
Graber: engraver
Greenspan: paint merchant
Haber: judge
Huberman: oat dealer
Hoffman: farmer
Kimmelman: grocer
Klinger: junk dealer
Kolatch: baker
Korn: grain dealer
Kratchmer: innkeeper
Kushner: furrier
Lapidus: gem engraver
Lehman: banker
Marmelstein: builder
Mass: bookseller
Mehlman: flour merchant
Messinger: brass dealer
Nager: carpenter
Netzky: baker
Packer: peddler

Pasternack: vegetable dealer
Plotkin: fish dealer
Portnoy: tailor
Rabinowitz: rabbi
Salzman: salt merchant
Saperstein: jeweler
Scharfstein: butcher
Schindler: roof shingler
Schlossman: locksmith
Schneider: tailor
Sherer: barber
Sherman: woolen-cloth dealer
Silverstein: jeweler
Spiegler: mirror maker
Steiner: jeweler
Tambor: drummer
Teller: barber
Tuchman: cloth merchant
Wasserman: water carrier
Wein: wine merchant
Zimmerman: carpenter
Zuckerman: candymaker
Zwirn: tailor

3 Consecration

Taking the First Steps in Jewish Learning

Do you remember learning to ride a bicycle? What about learning how to multiply fractions or play a musical instrument? What would have happened if you had never learned anything after you were three years old? Would you know how to tie your shoes? Would you be able to tell time?

Learning is a vital part of growing up, and Jewish learning is especially important because it tells us how to practice our religion and how to live according to God's commandments. In the first two chapters of this book, you learned about the commandments concerning the birth of a baby, and about the traditions of giving a child a Hebrew name.

Without Jewish learning, we would not know why we blow the shofar on Rosh Hashanah and why we eat matzah on Passover. We might not know the importance of asking forgiveness or giving tzedakah. And we would not know what it means to be Jewish and to live a Jewish life.

Because learning is so important, there is a ceremony to celebrate the first steps we take in our formal Jewish education. This ceremony is called Consecration.

The Consecration Ceremony

Long ago, when children began religious school, they received a small slate—a little blackboard—with the letters of the Hebrew alphabet written on it and covered with honey. As they recited the name of each letter, the children licked the honey. In this way, they experienced the sweetness of learning. Although we don't follow the same custom today, we do celebrate the beginning of a child's formal Jewish education.

The Consecration ceremony takes place at the beginning of the Jewish year (often during Simḥat Torah), which is also the beginning of the school year. In the synagogue the rabbi blesses all the children who are beginning their religious-school studies. These are the words of the blessing: "May God bless you and protect you. May God's face shine upon you and show you favor. May God's face be lifted to you and give you peace."

In many synagogues, each student who is consecrated receives a gift—often a prayerbook—from the congregation. The gift is a sign that the entire community recognizes the importance of Jewish learning.

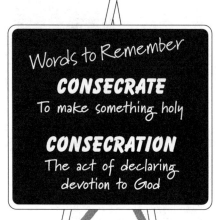

Words to Remember

CONSECRATE
To make something holy

CONSECRATION
The act of declaring devotion to God

Something to *Talk* About

Name three things you learned when you were younger that are still useful to you today.

Did you participate in a Consecration ceremony when you began your religious-school studies? *Did you receive a gift from the congregation? What was it?*

Why We Have a Consecration Ceremony

Imagine that you are building a house. If the foundation you build is strong, if the wood, bricks, and cement are of good quality, then the house will last. But if the foundation is weak, then the whole house will eventually topple over. Jewish education is like the foundation of a house. By giving children a Jewish education, we help to build a people who are strong and who will last.

In the Bible, the Book of Proverbs tells us, "Educate children in the way they should go, and even when they are old, they will not depart from it." Can you put this saying into your own words?

DID YOU KNOW?

Educating children has been important for much of Jewish history. Jewish schools have existed for more than two thousand years.

IT'S A FACT!

According to Jewish law, a community must build a school before it builds a synagogue.

What does this law say about the importance of teaching children in the Jewish community?

A Precious Gift

You will read many books in religious school, but the most important book you will read is the Torah, God's gift to the Jewish people. You already know many stories from the Torah, about Adam and Eve, Noah and the ark, and Abraham and Sarah.

The Torah also contains God's mitzvot. The mitzvot teach us how to lead good and honest lives. Although the Torah is thousands of years old, it says important things about every aspect of our lives today. Among many other things, the Torah teaches us to feed the hungry and clothe the homeless, to observe Shabbat and Jewish holidays, to care for our environment, to honor our parents, to pray, and to respect the rights of all people.

There is so much to learn from the Torah that some people spend their whole lives studying it. In fact, it is a mitzvah to study Torah. The Mishnah, a collection of rabbinic laws, contains this piece of wisdom about the Torah: "Turn it again and again, for everything is in it" (Avot 2:8).

Can you imagine risking your life to study Torah? Read this story to find out how one man risked his life.

Hillel was a poor man who lived in Jerusalem two thousand years ago. He spent all his spare time studying Torah. He saved his money to pay for lessons, but he couldn't always afford the tiny sum required to enter the house of study.

One Friday, on a cold winter afternoon, Hillel had no money at all. So eager was he to learn that he climbed up onto the roof to hear the wise words of the rabbis through the skylight. There Hillel listened to the teachers all afternoon. Even when snow began to fall, he remained on the rooftop.

The next morning the two rabbis, Shemaya and Avtalyon, noticed that the synagogue was unusually dark. When they went outside and looked up, they saw Hillel frozen on the rooftop! They carried him down, bathed him in warm water, and placed him near the fire. In this way, they saved Hillel's life.

From that day on, Hillel was permitted to enter the house of study without paying a fee for his lessons.

Hillel became one of our greatest rabbis. Perhaps you have read some of Rabbi Hillel's teachings. One of the most famous is: Do not do to other people what you would not want them to do to you. *Can you explain Hillel's teaching in your own words?*

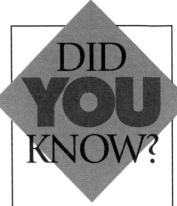

DID YOU KNOW?

We recite this prayer when we begin a session of Torah study: "Blessed are You, Adonai our God, Ruler of the world, who has made us holy with mitzvot and commanded us to study Torah."

Freedom to Learn

You might think that Jews have always had the freedom to go to religious school to study Torah and learn Hebrew and Jewish history. But this is a freedom we are actually very lucky to have. In some countries, Jews have not been allowed to study Judaism.

Until just a few years ago, for example, the government in Russia did not permit Jews to study Torah or teach their children our religious traditions. Even though disobeying this law was dangerous, many Russian Jews secretly studied Hebrew and celebrated Jewish holidays. They smuggled Hebrew prayerbooks (*siddurim*) into the country. Anyone discovered by the police to be engaged in these illegal activities was likely to be imprisoned.

In the last twenty years, more than half a million Jews left Russia and now enjoy religious freedom in the State of Israel and elsewhere in the world. Those who remain in Russia may now practice Judaism and study Torah more freely.

Something to Talk About

How did both Hillel and the Russian Jews demonstrate the importance of Jewish study?

It's a Mitzvah!

Jewish learning, called Talmud Torah in Hebrew, is a mitzvah. You might think that Talmud Torah refers only to studying the Torah, but the mitzvah involves all kinds of Jewish learning. When you learn to recite the blessings over the Ḥanukkah candles, you are doing the mitzvah of Talmud Torah. When you learn Hebrew, read a book about Israel, and sing Hebrew songs, you are also following the commandment of Talmud Torah. In fact, right now, as you study this book, you are performing the mitzvah.

Our tradition teaches that Talmud Torah is a most important mitzvah because study helps us to know how to live righteously. So that you may fulfill this important mitzvah, your parents have enrolled you in religious school.

List three things you have learned in religious school that will always be valuable to you.

1. _____

_____

2. _____

_____

3. _____

_____

_____

BUILDING JEWISH VALUES

Imagine that you are an architect. Your assignment is to construct a synagogue that will contain a sanctuary, a library, a social hall, and classrooms. On the diagram below, explain why each room should be included in the synagogue.

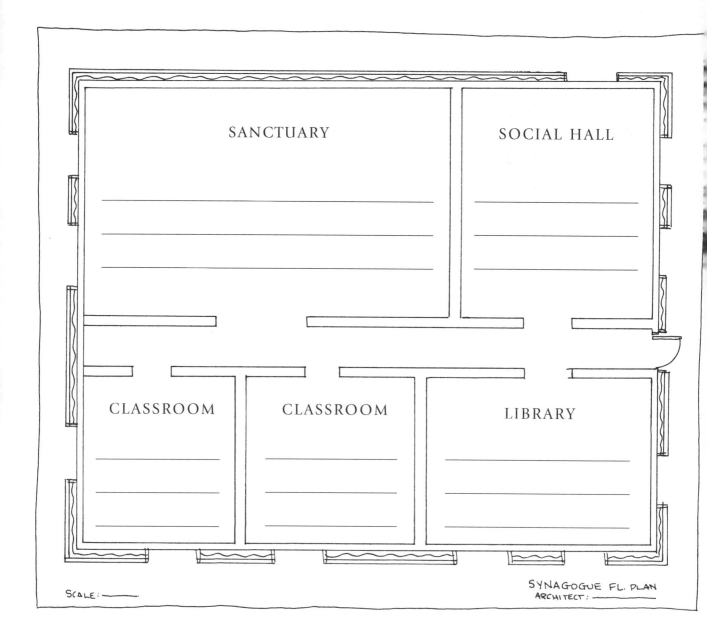

SANCTUARY

SOCIAL HALL

CLASSROOM

CLASSROOM

LIBRARY

SCALE: ———

SYNAGOGUE FL. PLAN
ARCHITECT: ———

IS IT IN THE TORAH?

Put a check next to each question you can learn to answer by studying Torah. Be prepared to explain your choices.

❏ 1. Will I hear the shofar sounded on Rosh Hashanah?

❏ 2. What time is it?

❏ 3. Am I being considerate?

❏ 4. How can I help poor people?

❏ 5. When should I feed my dog?

❏ 6. What should I put on the doorposts of my house to symbolize my relationship with God?

❏ 7. How should I spend my time on Shabbat?

❏ 8. What should I watch on television?

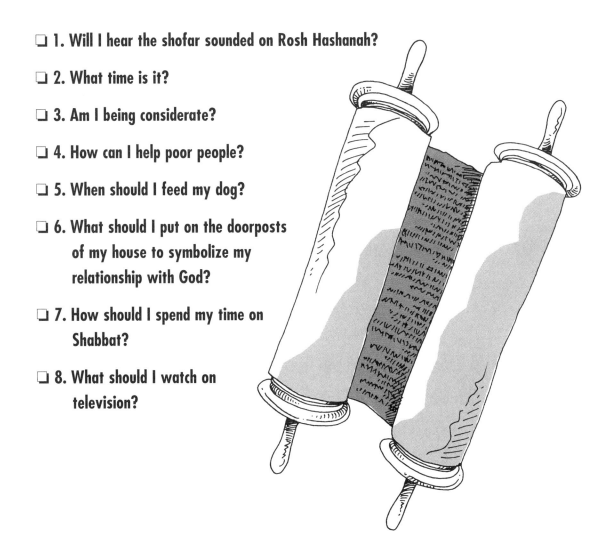

4

Bar Mitzvah
Bat Mitzvah

Becoming a Jewish Adult

What's the most important word in the phrases Bar Mitzvah and Bat Mitzvah? Mitzvah. Why? Because a mitzvah is a commandment from God. Without God's commandments — mitzvot — we wouldn't know what God wanted of us.

God's mitzvot are written in the Torah. If you counted all the mitzvot, you would find that there are 613 of them. Some mitzvot show us how to behave toward God. These mitzvot include lighting Shabbat candles, praying, attaching a mezuzah to our doorposts, and celebrating Jewish holidays. Other mitzvot show us how to behave toward other people. These commandments instruct us to feed the hungry, honor our parents, and respect the elderly.

When we are children, it is up to our parents to make sure that we perform the mitzvot. But at a certain age, Judaism tells us, we are old enough and wise enough to bear responsibility for our own behavior. When we reach this age, we become a Bar Mitzvah, a "Son of the Commandment," or a Bat Mitzvah, a "Daughter of the Commandment." To mark this event, we have a special ceremony.

The Age of a Bar Mitzvah or Bat Mitzvah

Traditionally a girl is responsible for fulfilling the mitzvot at the age of twelve years and one day, and a boy is responsible one year later. The earliest rabbis considered a thirteen-year-old boy and a twelve-year-old girl to be physically and emotionally mature and able to tell right from wrong. Today, the celebration marking a Bar Mitzvah or Bat Mitzvah takes place when a boy reaches the age of thirteen and a girl is twelve or thirteen.

You will be called to the Torah by your Hebrew name. Do you remember the form of your full Hebrew name? What is it?

Picking a Date

The date of your Bar Mitzvah or Bat Mitzvah ceremony will be chosen a year or even two years before your thirteenth birthday. The ceremony is usually held during Shabbat morning services. But, in fact, the ceremony may take place whenever the Torah is read publicly—for example, during Monday or Thursday morning services, on Shabbat afternoon, on certain holidays, or on the first day of a new Jewish month (Rosh Ḥodesh).

If you belong to a large congregation, several classmates may become eligible for their ceremony on the same Shabbat. When this happens, they may celebrate together.

Words to Remember

ALIYAH
The honor of being called to recite a blessing for the Torah reading

BAR MITZVAH
Son of the Commandment

BAT MITZVAH
Daughter of the Commandment

What Happens at the Ceremony

When you become a Bar Mitzvah or a Bat Mitzvah, you will be called up to the Torah for the first time. It is a great honor to recite the blessings before and after the Torah is read. This act of reciting the Torah blessings is known as an *aliyah*, which is Hebrew for "going up." It is called an *aliyah* because the person being honored goes up to the *bimah*, the platform from which the Torah is read. When you go up to the *bimah* for your first *aliyah*, you become an adult member of the Jewish community.

On the day of the ceremony, a Bar or Bat Mitzvah usually reads a section of the Torah portion, often the final section of the portion. A male who receives this honor is called *maftir*, a female is called *maftirah*. Both words are Hebrew for "one who concludes."

You will receive your first *aliyah* when you become a Bar Mitzvah or Bat Mitzvah. From that time on, you may receive an *aliyah* during any Torah service. As an adult, you may be honored with an *aliyah* on many occasions— for example, on a wedding anniversary, on the birth of a child, upon recovery from a serious illness, or on a *yahrzeit* (the anniversary of a loved one's death).

When you read from the Torah you will use a pointer called a yad—*Hebrew for "hand." The pointer allows you to follow the words without smearing the ink with your finger.*

Haftarah

A selection from one of the biblical books of the prophets is chanted after the Torah portion has been read. This selection is called the haftarah. A specific selection from a prophet, such as Isaiah, Jeremiah, or Ezekiel, is assigned to each Torah portion. The teaching of the prophet is related to the ideas in that Torah portion or to the time of the year.

Customarily, the person celebrating his Bar Mitzvah or her Bat Mitzvah chants the haftarah and the blessings beforehand and afterward. These haftarah blessings thank God for giving us the Torah, Shabbat, and the prophets.

Words to Remember

HAFTARAH
A reading from the prophets that concludes the Torah service

D'VAR TORAH, D'RASH
A short speech about the Torah portion or the haftarah

IT'S A FACT!

After you become a Bar Mitzvah or Bat Mitzvah, you can be counted in a *minyan,* the group of ten Jewish adults needed for public prayer.

D'var Torah

You may have an opportunity to speak to the congregation during the ceremony by delivering a *d'var Torah* or *d'rash*. This is a short speech about the Torah or haftarah portion and its connection to this important occasion.

DID **YOU** KNOW?

A *tallit* is a prayer shawl that is worn around the shoulders. A *tallit* has four corners and on each corner is a white knotted fringe. Wearing a *tallit* is a privilege and a mark of Jewish adulthood. A boy officially wears a *tallit* for the first time at his Bar Mitzvah ceremony. In congregations where prayer shawls are worn by women, a girl puts on a *tallit* for the first time at her Bat Mitzvah ceremony.

First Steps to Jewish Commitment

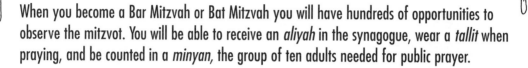

When you become a Bar Mitzvah or Bat Mitzvah you will have hundreds of opportunities to observe the mitzvot. You will be able to receive an *aliyah* in the synagogue, wear a *tallit* when praying, and be counted in a *minyan,* the group of ten adults needed for public prayer.

Here are twelve mitzvot that you can begin to fulfill right now, and practical suggestions for observing them. *Can you think of other ways to fulfill these mitzvot?*

1. Ahavat Tzion (Love of Israel)
Contribute some of your allowance money to the Jewish National Fund to plant a tree in Israel.

2. Bal Tash'ḥit (Caring for the Environment)
Turn off the lights when you leave a room.

3. Bikkur Ḥolim (Visiting the Sick)
Bring a homework assignment to an ill classmate.

4. Hachnasat Orḥim (Welcoming Guests)
Invite a friend for Friday night dinner.

5. Hiddur P'nai Zaken
(Showing Respect for the Aged)
Run an errand for an elderly neighbor.

6. Kibbud Av Va-Em (Honoring Parents)
Take on a new chore at home.

7. Ma'achil R'evim (Feeding the Hungry)
Contribute canned goods to a food drive.

8. Rodef Shalom (Pursuing Peace)
Settle an argument between friends.

9. Sh'mirat Shabbat (Observing Shabbat)
Light Shabbat candles on Friday evening.

10. Talmud Torah (Learning Torah)
Visit a Jewish museum or exhibition.

11. Tefillah (Praying)
Recite the Shema before going to sleep.

12. Tza'ar Ba'alei Ḥayyim
(Kindness to Animals)
Avoid buying and using products that have been tested on animals in inhumane experiments.

Preparing for the Ceremony

By attending religious school, you are already preparing for your Bar Mitzvah or Bat Mitzvah celebration. You are learning about Jewish customs and ceremonies. You are studying Jewish history and the Bible. And you are learning Hebrew so that you will be able to read the Torah, chant the haftarah, and join the rest of the congregation when prayers are recited in Hebrew.

By attending your synagogue's services during the months before your Bar Mitzvah or Bat Mitzvah ceremony, you will become more familiar and more comfortable with the customs of your congregation.

Also during that time, your cantor or rabbi will teach you your Torah and haftarah readings. Your rabbi will help you write a *d'var Torah.* And you will have the chance to participate in meaningful acts of tzedakah to help people who are less fortunate than you.

Your Bar Mitzvah or Bat Mitzvah is more than a ceremony in the synagogue. And it is much more than a party in your honor. Bar Mitzvah or Bat Mitzvah is something you become—a responsible Jewish adult, one who knows to follow the teachings of Judaism. You will not become a Bat Mitzvah or a Bar Mitzvah for one day or for one year. You will become a Bar Mitzvah or a Bat Mitzvah—a Jewish adult—for your entire life.

Jigsaw Puzzle

Use the words in the puzzle pieces to complete the sentences.

On the day of your Bar or Bat _____, you receive an

_____, read your _____ portion, and give a

_____ Torah. Most important, you understand your

_____ to fulfill the mitzvot. After the ceremony, you

may be counted in a _____.

It's a Mitzvah!

Write the name of the mitzvah that is being performed in each picture. Choose from the mitzvot in the box below. To help you remember each mitzvah, turn to page 48.

Hiddur P'nai Zaken	**Tefillah**
Bikkur Ḥolim	**Hachnasat Orḥim**
Tza'ar Ba'alei Ḥayyim	**Ma'achil R'evim**
Bal Tash'ḥit	**Ahavat Tzion**

_____

_____

_____

5 Confirmation

Graduating from Religious School

The older you become, the more you need to know. Think about it. When you were in second grade, perhaps the only Hebrew you knew was the letters of the alphabet. And that was enough to know at that age. But soon it was time for you to ask the Four Questions on Passover, so you began to learn to read Hebrew. In just a few years, you will need to learn to chant the haftarah portion for your Bar Mitzvah or Bat Mitzvah ceremony. And many years from now, when you are old enough to have a family of your own, you will want to know how to hang a mezuzah on the doorpost of your house, lead a Passover seder, and build a sukkah.

Jewish learning is a lifelong journey of discovery. Just as we continue to learn about subjects like math, history, and music even after we complete high school, we continue to study about Judaism even after we complete religious school.

The completion of any important activity—especially one involving hard work—is usually a time for celebration. The completion of high school, for example, is marked by a graduation ceremony. In the same way, in many congregations, the completion of religious school is marked by a Confirmation ceremony.

Confirmation

Students who have become a Bat Mitzvah or Bar Mitzvah often continue their formal Jewish schooling. They may attend a Jewish high school once or twice a week, or the students may study together with the rabbi of the congregation or with the principal of the religious school. They learn what Judaism has to say about many important and complex issues. Some of these issues are practical—how to build a loving personal relationship and how to care for the environment. Some of these issues involve ideas—do bad things happen to good people and what happens after a person dies.

This period of study usually lasts for two years. Then a formal graduation ceremony is held. The ceremony is called Confirmation.

The Confirmation ceremony usually takes place on Shavuot, the holiday that celebrates God's giving the Torah to the Israelites at Mount Sinai. This is an appropriate time for Confirmation. For just as the ancient Israelites stood as a community at the foot of Mount Sinai to receive the Torah, so the members of a Confirmation class stand together before the Holy Ark to declare their commitment to God's teachings and the Jewish community.

Words to Remember

JEWISH COMMUNITY
A group of Jewish people who live, work, study, and pray together

CONFIRMATION
The act of formally recognizing students' loyalty to their religion

Do you know the difference between a Bar Mitzvah or a Bat Mitzvah ceremony and Confirmation? A Bar Mitzvah or Bat Mitzvah ceremony takes place at age twelve or thirteen. The ceremony welcomes the boy or girl as a member of the Jewish community and marks the beginning of Jewish adulthood.

Confirmation takes place at age fifteen or sixteen. The ceremony is celebrated by an entire class and marks the conclusion of the students' formal religious-school education.

From the Midrash

SONG *of* SONGS
RABBAH 1:4

The Jewish people made a Covenant with God at Mount Sinai. Read this legend to find out what they offered as a guarantee.

When the people of Israel stood at Mount Sinai, ready to receive the Torah, God said to them, "Before I give you My Torah, you must give Me something that proves you will use it wisely."

What could the Israelites offer in exchange for this precious gift?

First the people offered jewelry: bracelets and rings, necklaces and pins. But God said that the Torah is more precious than all the jewels in the world.

The people thought again and offered God our biblical ancestors as proof that they would use the Torah wisely. But God refused them too.

Finally, the people promised to teach their children, and all generations of children after them, to love and obey God's commandments. God was pleased and said, "That is a good promise. For the sake of your children, I will give you the Torah."

Something to Talk About

Why do you think God accepted the third promise? What three things can you do to keep this promise?

Becoming a Jewish Leader

Confirmation prepares you to become a Jewish leader. Confirmation study helps determine the values and issues that are important. With this information, you can develop a vision of your own future and the future of the Jewish people. You can learn to be true to yourself, to understand who you are, and to make ethical decisions based on the Jewish ideas of right and wrong. This knowledge will give you the courage to act, and the ability to inspire others.

Something to  About

When we declare our commitment to Judaism, we recognize our connection to all Jewish people everywhere. This idea is called K'lal Yisrael, "all the people of Israel." We show our concern for K'lal Yisrael by remembering that all Jews are responsible for one another no matter where they live.

Many of the people we read about in the Bible demonstrated their commitment to K'lal Yisrael. One example is Queen Esther, whose story we read on Purim. As you know, Esther risked her life to save the Jews of Persia. Can you think of another person in the Bible whose actions demonstrated a passionate concern for K'lal Yisrael?

What can you do to show your commitment to K'lal Yisrael? How can working with other members of the Jewish community help you honor this important value?

Word Identification

Explain how each word is connected to Confirmation.

1. Graduation _____

2. Shavuot _____

3. Study _____

4. Mount Sinai _____

5. Leadership _____
_____

What's More Important?

Many years ago the rabbis tried to decide which is more important—studying Torah or living according to the laws of Torah (for example, by observing Shabbat).

Rabbi Tarfon thought following the laws of Torah is more important. Rabbi Akiba argued that the only way to learn the meaning of the laws is to study Torah. Therefore studying Torah is more important than living according to its laws.

Which do you think is more important—studying Torah or living according to the laws of Torah? Why?

In the end, the rabbis decided that studying Torah is more important when it leads to living according to the laws of Torah.

Do you agree with the rabbis' decision? Explain your answer.

6

The Marriage Ceremony

Beginning a Jewish Family

Family traditions add extra meaning to our Jewish customs. Are there special customs in your family? Do they give a particular meaning to your celebration of the holidays? For example, do the Shabbat candles seem to glow especially warmly because your mother lights them in candlesticks that once belonged to your great-grandmother? Do the matzah balls at your Passover seder taste better than others because your father follows his grandmother's recipe when he makes them?

Customs and traditions are passed from one generation to the next, from grandmother to grandson, from father to daughter, from aunt to cousin. This process keeps Judaism alive. That is why the family is very important in Jewish life.

The creation of a new family begins with a wedding. When two people marry, they set up a new Jewish home, a place where they will share holidays and life-cycle events with other family members and with friends. Because the wedding ceremony celebrates the continuation of the Jewish family, it is one of the happiest of all life-cycle events.

Before the Wedding

When two people fall in love and decide to marry, there are several things they must do. They must choose a date for the wedding, meet with the rabbi who will perform the ceremony, decide where the wedding will be held, and invite their guests. Although preparations for a wedding often begin many months before the ceremony takes place, the wedding celebration itself begins on the Shabbat before the wedding day.

In some communities the groom *(ḥatan)* and the bride *(kallah)* are called to the Torah during the Shabbat service. This special *aliyah* is known as an *aufruf*, which is Yiddish for "calling up." The bride and groom recite the blessings before and after the Torah reading. Sometimes congregants shower the couple with soft candies as a way of wishing them a sweet life together. Sometimes the congregants sing a song in the couple's honor. In other congregations, the bride and groom are called to the *bimah* and stand in front of the Ark, where the rabbi recites a special prayer for the couple's happiness.

In either case, the Jewish community publicly expresses its good wishes.

A happy event, such as a wedding, is called a *simḥah,* Hebrew for "joy."
What other Jewish life-cycle event have you learned about that you would also call a simḥah?

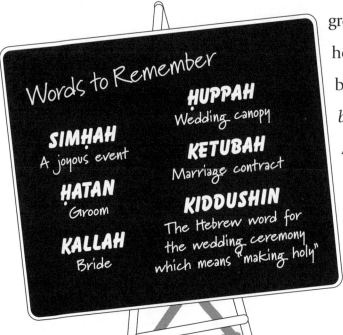

Words to Remember

SIMḤAH
A joyous event

HATAN
Groom

KALLAH
Bride

HUPPAH
Wedding canopy

KETUBAH
Marriage contract

KIDDUSHIN
The Hebrew word for the wedding ceremony which means "making holy"

What Makes a Jewish Wedding Different?

Two things that make a Jewish wedding different from all others are the *ḥuppah* and the *ketubah*.

The *ḥuppah* is a wedding canopy. At a Jewish wedding, the bride and groom stand under it during the ceremony. The *ḥuppah* is made of fine cloth, such as silk or velvet, and is hung like a small tent from four poles. Sometimes a *tallit* serves as a *ḥuppah*. The poles are often decorated with flowers and leaves.

DID YOU KNOW?

Some people say that the ḥuppah *is a symbol of the special tent where the bride and groom spent their wedding night in the days of the Bible. Others say that it is a symbol of the Jewish home the couple will build together.*

The *ketubah* is a Jewish marriage contract. The *ketubah* expresses the bride and groom's spiritual commitment to one another. In it, the bride and groom promise to take care of each other and to make a Jewish home together. The *ketubah* includes the date and the place of the wedding and the Hebrew names of the bride and the groom.

IT'S A FACT!

The *ketubah* has been used by Jewish brides and grooms for more than two thousand years. Traditionally, the *ketubah* was written in Aramaic, the language Jews spoke in ancient Babylonia. Today, the *ketubah* is often written in Hebrew. A *ketubah* may also have an English translation.

day of the month
year 57 _____
_____ 19 _____
_____ant of Marriage was entered
_____ between
the Bridegroom _____,
and his Bride _____

The said Bridegroom made the following declaration to his Bride:
"Be thou my wife according to the law of Moses and Israel. I faithfully promise that I will be a true husband unto thee. I will honor and cherish thee, protect and support thee, and provide all that is necessary for thy sustenance, even as it becometh a Jewish husband to do. I also take upon myself all such further obligations for thy maintenance as are prescribed by our religious statute."
And the said Bride has plighted her troth unto him, in affection and sincerity, and has thus taken upon herself the fulfillment of all the duties incumbent upon a Jewish wife.
This Covenant of Marriage was duly executed and witnessed this day, according to the customs of Israel.

Rabbi _____
Bride _____
Bridegroom _____
Witness _____
Witness _____

ב _____ לחדש _____ בשבת
שנת חמשת אלפים שבע מאות _____ לבריאת עולם
למנין שאנו מונין כאן _____ במדינת
אמעריקא הצפונית איך החתן _____ בר
המכונה _____ אמר לה להדא
בת _____ המכונה _____ הוי לי לאנתו
כדת משה וישראל ואנא אפלח ואוקיר ואיזון ואפרנס יתיכי
ליכי כהלכות גוברין יהודאין דפלחין ומוקרין וזנין
ומפרנסין לנשיהון בקושטא ויהיבנא ליכי מוהר
כסף זוזי _____ דחזי ליכי _____ ומזוניכי
וכסותיכי וסיפוקיכי ומיעל לותיכי כאורח כל ארעא
וצביאת מרת _____ דא והוית ליה לאנתו ודין
_____ עלת ליה מבי _____ בין בכסף בין בזהב
_____ ני דלבושא בשימושי דירה ובשימושי
חתן דנן _____
חתן דנן והוסיף _____
_____ ים כסף צרוף אחרים כנגדן
_____ וך אמר _____
_____ נדוניא דין ותוספתא
_____ להתפרע מן כל שפר
_____ בל שמיא דקנאי ודעתיד
_____ יות ודלית להון אחריות
_____ פרוע מנהון שטר כתובתא
_____ נאי ואפילו מן גלימא דעל
_____ א דין ולעלם ואחריות וחומר
_____ דין ותוספתא דא קבל עליו
_____ שטרי כתובות ותוספתות דנהגין בבנת
_____ עסיין כתקון חכמינו זכרונם לברכה דלא
כאסמכתא ודלא כטופסי דשטרי וקנינא מן
בר _____ חתן דנן למרת
בת _____ דא על כל מה דכתוב ומפורש
לעיל במנא דכשר למקניא ביה והכל שריר וקים:

נאום _____ עד _____
ונאום _____ עד _____

The Wedding Ceremony

The bride and groom are escorted to the *huppah* by their parents, and the wedding ceremony begins. The rabbi recites a blessing over the wine, and the bride and groom each take a sip.

Next the bride and groom exchange rings. As they do this, they recite these ancient words: "By this ring you are consecrated to me according to the law of Moses and Israel." The circle of the ring is a symbol of the continuous, unending love the bride and groom have for each other.

After the ring ceremony, the rabbi reads the *ketubah* aloud. Then the rabbi talks to the couple about the meaning of marriage and its holiness.

It is now time for the reading of the Seven Blessings. Usually only one blessing is recited when we fulfill a mitzvah, such as lighting Shabbat candles, hanging a mezuzah, or eating a meal. But at a wedding, we recite seven blessings. They are called *Shevah Brachot*. These blessings are usually recited or chanted by the rabbi or the cantor.

The Seven Blessings thank God for creating wine, the universe, and people. After the seventh blessing, which asks God to bring joy and gladness to the bride and groom, the

It's a Mitzvah!

Some couples share their wedding flowers with hospital patients and give left-over food to the needy in the community.

There are Jewish laws concerning the rings used at a wedding ceremony:

1. The ring must be made of a solid metal. Usually gold is used.
2. The ring cannot have any jewels or stones in it.

The reason for these laws is that Jews believe marriage should be a continuous, uninterrupted partnership.

couple sip wine from the Kiddush cup. The rabbi then declares the couple married in accordance with both Jewish and civil law, and the rabbi blesses them as they stand with heads bowed.

Then the groom does something very unusual. A glass wrapped in a cloth is placed on the floor, and the groom crushes it under his foot.

Afterwards, the wedding guests shout "Mazal Tov! Good Luck!" In some congregations, the bride may break the glass as well.

The ceremony has ended, but the celebration continues with music and dancing, food and singing. Sometimes the bride and groom are lifted on chairs and carried around the room during this joyful *simḥah*.

It's a Mitzvah!

Nothing should interfere with the act of helping a bride and groom celebrate their wedding. Even if you are studying the Torah, the rabbis said, when a wedding procession passes your window, you should put aside your books and join in the celebration.

Why Do We Smash a Glass?

Some people say that the breaking of a glass at the wedding ceremony reminds us of one of the saddest times in our people's history: the destruction of the Temple in Jerusalem. Others say that the glass is broken to remind us that even at our happiest celebrations, we should not forget that there will be moments of sadness in our future.

Long ago in many Jewish communities a wedding was celebrated for a whole week. For seven days, the bride and groom would be invited to the homes of friends and family members for lunch and dinner. The Seven Blessings, *Shevah Brachot,* were repeated at the end of each of these meals. Some couples continue this tradition today.

The first marriage described in the Bible is between Rebecca and Isaac. Read this story to find out how Isaac's wife was chosen.

Abraham decided it was time for his son, Isaac, to marry. He spoke to his most trusted servant, Eliezer.

"Go to the city where my brother Nahor lives," he instructed Eliezer. "There you will find a wife for Isaac."

"How will I know her?" Eliezer asked, wondering what sort of woman Isaac would like.

"God will point her out to you," Abraham replied.

So Eliezer saddled ten camels, loaded them with gifts, and set out across the desert. When he reached the city where Nahor lived, he led the camels to the well. There he saw many young women filling their jars with water.

"So many women!" Eliezer thought. "How will I choose the right one?" But then he remembered Abraham's words.

"Please, God," he prayed, "help me find a good wife for Isaac."

At that moment, Eliezer noticed a beautiful young woman with a clay pitcher on her shoulder. He approached her and asked if he might drink some water from her jar, for he had just completed a long trip across the desert.

IT'S A FACT!

Some people say that brides wear veils because it is written in the Bible that at Rebecca's wedding, "Rebecca took a veil and covered herself with it."

"Of course, my lord," the young woman replied. And before he could thank her, she continued, "Your camels must also be thirsty." And she went to the well and drew more water, until all the animals were satisfied.

"What is your name?" Eliezer asked.

"I am Rebecca, the daughter of Bethuel, the son of Nahor," she answered.

Eliezer smiled. He knew that God had helped him find the perfect wife for Isaac.

Something to Talk About

Why did Rebecca give water to Eliezer? Did Rebecca wait for Eliezer to ask before she gave water to his camels? How did these actions show Eliezer that this was the woman God had chosen to be Isaac's wife?

Match Ups

Draw a line from the word on the left to its definition on the right.

1. Shevah Brachot

2. ketubah

3. ḥuppah

4. ḥatan

5. kallah

6. aufruf

7. kiddushin

wedding canopy

wedding ceremony

marriage contract

groom

aliyah for the bride and
groom before their wedding

Seven Blessings recited
during the wedding ceremony

bride

What Do You Do?

The newly married couple will celebrate the holidays together in their home. Each family celebrates the holidays a little differently.

Describe how your family celebrates these Jewish holidays:

1. **Sukkot:** *Do you build a sukkah? What do you do inside a sukkah?*

2. **Rosh Hashanah:** *Does your family send New Year cards? Do you make them or buy them?*

3. **Ḥanukkah:** *How many ḥanukkiot do you light? In what room do you light candles?*

4. **Passover:** *What special foods does your family prepare on Passover?*

Complete the
Ketubah

Interview someone in your family to discover information about his or her wedding.

Record it in the *ketubah* below.

Many couples' *ketubot* are decorated with colorful art. Decorate this *ketubah*.

_____
Groom's Name

and

_____
Bride's Name

were united in marriage

in _____
Name of City

on the _____ day of _____
Day   Month

in the year _____

according to the laws of the State of _____

and in accordance with the customs of Israel by

_____
Rabbi's Name

_____   _____
Witness's Name   Witness's Name

7 The Funeral

Saying Good-bye

Imagine that you are getting ready to move to a new city. The moving van will soon arrive. The boxes are packed, and you've said good-bye to all your friends. But it is difficult to leave. You wonder what your new neighborhood will be like. You worry and feel a bit scared.

In a way, death is like that unknown neighborhood. It is a mystery, and it can be frightening because no one knows what happens after we die.

Our Jewish tradition understands that we are never ready to lose someone we love. To help us through this difficult experience, to help us honor the person who has died, and to comfort us during a very sad time, Judaism provides a series of rituals and customs.

Before the Funeral

A Jewish person is buried as soon after death as possible, usually within twenty-four hours.

The staff of the funeral parlor or members of a Jewish burial society called the *ḥevrah kaddisha*, are specially trained to prepare the body for burial. They wash and dry it. Then they wrap it in a white shroud, or burial garment, made of cotton or linen, or in a favorite suit or dress. This ritual washing is called *taharah*. Just as babies are washed when they enter the world, so people who have died leave the world cleansed.

To show our respect for the person who has died, we never leave the body alone from the time of death until the time of burial. This ritual of staying with the body is called *shemirah* ("watching" or "guarding"). Those who keep watch recite prayers and psalms.

Jewish funerals do not take place on Shabbat, on the festivals of Passover, Shavuot, and Sukkot, or on the High Holy Days.

The Coffin

A coffin is a box in which a body is buried. At Jewish funerals, the coffin is usually made of plain wood. It may be constructed with nails, but traditional coffins are held together with wooden pegs. Sometimes a bag filled

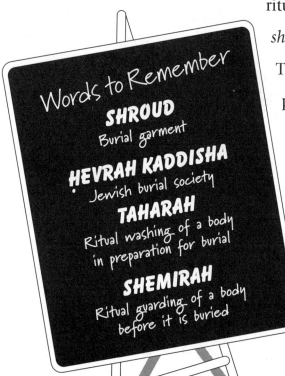

Words to Remember

SHROUD
Burial garment

ḤEVRAH KADDISHA
Jewish burial society

TAHARAH
Ritual washing of a body in preparation for burial

SHEMIRAH
Ritual guarding of a body before it is buried

with soil from Israel is placed under the head, or some of the soil
may be sprinkled over the
body. The coffin usually
remains closed. Our reli-
gion discourages looking
at the body.

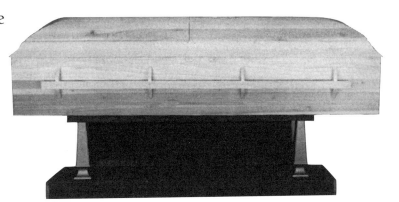

The Funeral Service

Jewish funerals are short and simple. The service usually takes place
in a funeral chapel or in the synagogue. Sometimes the service is
performed next to the grave, in the cemetery.

Before the funeral service begins, close relatives (parents, children,
the spouse, or siblings of the person who has died) perform an act
called *keriah*. *Keriah* is a Hebrew word meaning "tearing." It refers to
the act of tearing clothing or cutting a black ribbon that is pinned
to clothing. This is a way of showing the pain we feel when we have
lost someone we love. Tearing our clothes reflects the feeling that the
person who has died has been "torn away." The torn garment or ribbon
is traditionally worn for seven days.

The rabbi may read several psalms at the beginning of the funeral
service. The one most commonly recited is Psalm 23. This is how it
begins:

Adonai is my shepherd, I shall not want.
Adonai makes me lie down in green pastures,
leads me beside still waters,
and restores my soul.
You lead me in right paths
for the sake of Your name.
Even when I walk in the valley of the
shadow of death,
I shall fear no evil,
for You are with me.

This psalm declares our belief in God's power and in God's concern for those who have died. Why do you think this psalm is often recited at funerals?

The Eulogy

During the funeral service, the rabbi, relatives, or a close friend talks about the person who has died. This speech is called a eulogy (in Hebrew a *hesped*). The speaker tells about the person's life, recounts his or her good deeds, and shares special memories. Sometimes the eulogy contains amusing stories about the person or his or her interests. Sometimes the speech is sad. What is most important is that the eulogy helps the mourners lovingly remember the person who has died.

When you see someone wearing a black ribbon pinned to his or her clothing, what does it mean? What might you say or do to make this person feel less sad?

The funeral service concludes with the prayer El Malei Raḥamim ("God, Full of Compassion"). This prayer asks God to grant peace and protection of the soul of the person who has died.

Burial and the Kaddish

The coffin is brought to the cemetery. After the coffin has been lowered into the grave, relatives and friends may help cover the coffin with a handful or a shovelful of earth. It is a mitzvah to help fill the grave. This is a difficult mitzvah to perform, but it is also one of the most important. By helping to fill the grave, we help create a safe and proper resting place.

A mourner recites Kaddish in the presence of a *minyan,* a group of at least ten adult Jews. When a parent dies, the son or daughter may recite Kaddish for eleven months.

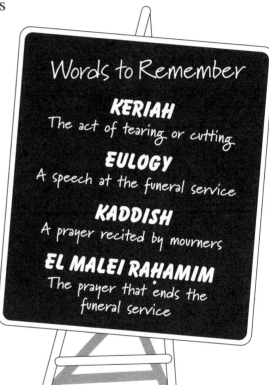

Words to Remember

KERIAH
The act of tearing or cutting

EULOGY
A speech at the funeral service

KADDISH
A prayer recited by mourners

EL MALEI RAHAMIM
The prayer that ends the funeral service

After the grave has been filled with earth, the Kaddish is recited. Although this prayer is recited at every funeral, the words of the Kaddish do not refer to death. Instead, the words of the Kaddish praise God's glory and holiness, which endure forever. The prayer asks for peace for us and for all the people of Israel.

From the Midrash

ECCLESIASTES
RABBAH 7:4

*What lesson does this midrash teach us
about birth and death?*

When a person is born, everyone celebrates. When a person dies, everyone cries. But should it be this way?

When babies are born, no one knows how their lives will turn out. Will
they be good people or evil? Will their lives be productive or wasteful? But
when people die, we can rejoice if their lives have been good, if they have
made the world a better place because they were here.

Our rabbis taught that when we think about death, we should imagine two ships in a harbor. One is leaving port; the other is returning. Many people cheer the ship that leaves the harbor, but few notice the ship that returns.

A wise man said, "There is no reason to rejoice over the ship that is leaving. For no one knows the storms it may encounter on its voyage. But we should all cheer the ship that is sailing back into the harbor, because it has returned safely!"

Something to Talk About

What does the ship leaving the harbor stand for? What does the returning ship symbolize? What lessons does this midrash teach us?

True or False?

Mark each true sentence with a T. Put an F next to each sentence that is false.

1. ___ We show respect for the dead by waiting seven days to bury them.

2. ___ During the funeral, the coffin remains open.

3. ___ It is a mitzvah to help bury someone.

4. ___ A Jewish funeral can take place on Yom Kippur.

5. ___ *Keriah* is a Hebrew word meaning "washing."

6. ___ A speech at a funeral service is called a eulogy.

7. ___ *Taharah* is the ritual washing of the body.

8. ___ The ritual guarding of the body is called Kaddish.

9. ___ A Jewish coffin is made of steel.

10. ___ When a parent dies, the child may recite Kaddish for eleven months.

What's Miss ng?

Fill in the missing words.

1. The Kaddish does not refer to _____

2. A burial garment is called a _____

3. The *ḥevrah kaddisha* is a Jewish _____

4. A _____ is a box in which a body is buried.

5. Kaddish is recited only in the presence of a _____

Ethical Wills

A will is a legal document that explains what should happen to the money and other possessions people leave when they die.

Some people also write an ethical will. This special document contains a person's most important beliefs. By writing an ethical will, a person can offer guidance and comfort after death to those he or she loved.

A famous Yiddish author, Shalom Aleichem, wrote an ethical will for his children. Here is part of it:

> *My wish is that my children guard their mama, enhance her older years, sweeten her bitter life, heal her broken heart. Don't cry when you remember me, but rather remember me with joy. But the main thing is to live together in harmony... help each other in bad times; take pity on a poor person. Children, carry with honor my hard-earned Jewish name and may God in Heaven help you. Amen.*

Which part of this ethical will is most important to you?
Why? _____

_____

_____

_____

8 Rituals of Mourning

······································

Remembering Those We Love

It hurts when you fall off a bicycle and scrape your knee. The cut may bleed, and you might even cry because it hurts so much. You or your mom or dad puts medicine on the wound so it won't become infected. Then you cover it with a bandage to keep it clean. For the next couple of days, your knee may be sore when you bend it. But over time the bruise begins to heal, and soon you can go bike riding again.

When someone we love dies, the hurt we feel is much deeper and much more painful than the hurt we feel when we cut ourselves. But the process of healing is similar. At the beginning, the pain is very strong. The loss we feel hurts a lot. But over time the hurt becomes less painful.

To help people heal and to make the loss of a loved one less difficult, Jewish tradition defines three periods of mourning: the first week after the burial, the first month after the burial, and the first twelve months after the burial. Step by step, little by little, our Jewish rituals help us to live through difficult days until we can finally return to normal, everyday life.

The First Week of Mourning

Immediately after the burial, a period of mourning begins. It is called *shiva*, the Hebrew word for "seven." Shiva is observed by close relatives — those who have lost a parent, child, husband, wife, brother, or sister.

The practice of *shiva* probably dates back to the time of the Bible. When Jacob died, his son Joseph mourned for seven days.

Upon returning home from the cemetery, the mourners light a special candle. This candle burns for seven days, the length of the *shiva* period. The light of the candle is a symbol of God's presence in the house of mourning.

Words to Remember

MOURNER
A person whose close relative has recently died

SHIVA
The seven-day mourning period that begins after a funeral

KADDISH
Prayer recited by mourners

For seven days or, in some families, for just two or three days, the mourners do not go to work. They stay at home. Friends and relatives visit them to show their love and to give their support. Prayer services are held in the home so mourners can recite the Kaddish.

There are many interesting practices related to the mourning process. For example, during the *shiva* period, mourners often sit on low, hard benches or stools. This is where the phrase "sitting shiva" comes from. The reason

After returning from a cemetery, many people rinse their hands before they enter the mourners' house. They do this to show that they have left the world of death behind and are about to enter the home of the living.

for their doing this may be found in the biblical story of Job. In this story, Job's whole family has died, and three friends come to comfort Job. They sit "beside him on the ground seven days and seven nights."

Mourners do not concern themselves with their appearance during the *shiva* period. Many women do not wear makeup, and many men do not shave. Mirrors in the house of mourning may be covered with cloths or sheets.

When *shiva* is over, many people end this first period of mourning by taking a walk around the block. This symbolizes their return to a more normal life.

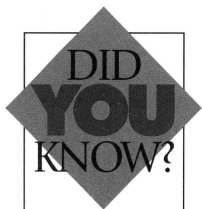

Neighbors and friends usually prepare a meal for the mourners when they return from the cemetery. This meal is called a **seudat havra'ah,** *a "meal of condolence." The meal often includes foods that are round, such as bagels and hard-boiled eggs. Roundness is a symbol of the circle of life.*

94

The gravestone, or monument (*matzevah* in Hebrew), may lie flat on the ground or stand vertically. The stone is engraved with the name of the deceased in Hebrew and English and the dates of birth and death. Often five Hebrew letters appear on the tombstone: ת, נ, צ, ב, ה. They stand for the Hebrew words meaning "May her or his soul be bound up in the bond of eternal life."

The First Month of Mourning

The next stage of mourning is called *sheloshim* (Hebrew for "thirty"). It lasts for thirty days from the time of the funeral. Some people say we mourn for thirty days because the ancient Israelites mourned for Moses for thirty days after he died.

During this first month, mourners return to a more normal routine. Adults return to work, and children go back to school. Still, mourners usually do not attend parties and other social events. Often they will go to the synagogue each day to recite the Kaddish prayer. Kaddish for a parent is recited for eleven months from the time of the funeral. After *sheloshim*, only those who have lost a parent are still considered mourners.

Some people donate money to plant trees in Israel in memory of a person who has died. Others give money to charity—tzedakah—in memory of the person.

It's a Mitzvah!

It's a mitzvah to comfort a mourner, especially during the shiva period. Visits may be made during the day or in the evening. When you visit, don't worry about what to say. What is important is being there, giving a hug, and showing that you care. By doing this you provide comfort to someone who has lost a loved one.

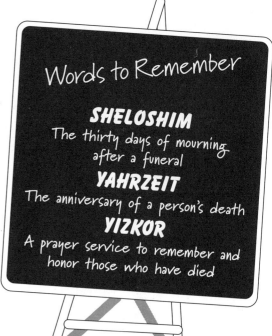

Words to Remember

SHELOSHIM
The thirty days of mourning after a funeral

YAHRZEIT
The anniversary of a person's death

YIZKOR
A prayer service to remember and honor those who have died

The Unveiling

The monument that marks the site of the grave is dedicated at the end of *shiva* or up to twelve months after death. During this ceremony, called an unveiling, a cloth or veil covering the tombstone is removed. A brief prayer service is held, the person's life is remembered, and Kaddish is recited. The unveiling often marks the end of the mourning period.

Have you seen a plaque like this in your synagogue? It is often hung on a wall in the sanctuary or in the entrance hall of the building. Each brass plaque is engraved with the name of a member of the congregation, or a relative of a member, who has died. These memorial plaques honor the memories of people who are no longer with us. On some plaques electric bulbs are placed next to each person's name. These memorial lights are lit on the anniversary of the person's death. The light is called *ner neshama*, "the light of the soul." During Friday evening and Shabbat morning services, it is also customary to read aloud the names of people whose *yahrzeit* is being remembered during the coming week.

Yahrzeit and Yizkor

After the unveiling, the period of mourning may be officially over, but our memories of loved ones never end. So Judaism gives us opportunities each year to honor their memories.

The anniversary of a person's death is called a *yahrzeit.* Every year, on the anniversary of a loved one's death (according to the Jewish calendar), we remember and honor him or her by reciting Kaddish in the synagogue and by lighting a memorial candle. This *yahrzeit* candle burns for twenty-four hours. Many people also visit the grave.

A special service in the synagogue, called Yizkor (Hebrew for "May God Remember"), gives us another opportunity to remember and honor our deceased relatives and friends. The Yizkor service takes place on several holidays: Passover, Shavuot, Sukkot, and Yom Kippur.

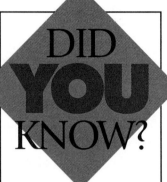

DID YOU KNOW?

When people visit a grave, they often leave a small stone or pebble on the monument to show that they were there. The stone is a symbol of the bond between the visitor and the person who has died.

Something to Talk About

Jewish traditions and customs help us remember those who are no longer alive. The memories of friends and relatives who have died will always be with us. The things they taught us continue to guide us as we go on with our lives. *What have you learned from your parents or grandparents? What qualities do you want to be remembered for?*

Match Ups

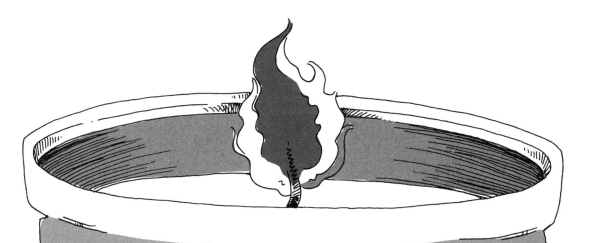

Draw a line from the word on the left to its definition on the right.

1. yahrzeit

2. Yizkor

3. shiva

4. mourner

5. sheloshim

6. unveiling

7. seudat havra'ah

8. Kaddish

first week of mourning

dedication of the gravestone
or monument

first month of mourning

synagogue service to remember
relatives and friends who have died

person whose close relative has
recently died

first meal eaten after returning
from the cemetery

anniversary of a person's death

prayer recited by mourners

Making a Shiva Call

It is a mitzvah to visit a house of mourning during the *shiva* period. The purpose of the visit is to offer friendship and sympathy to the mourners.

Read the following list of things you might do when making a *shiva* call. Then add some of your own ideas.

Give the mourner a hug.

Listen carefully to what the mourner says.

Bring a gift of food.

Share a personal memory about the person who has died.

Participate in the prayer service, if there is one.

What other things can you do?

_____

_____

_____

_____

Reading a Jewish Tombstone

On the tombstone:

תנצבה
ABRAHAM
KANTOWITZ
אברהם בן אדם ורבקה

February 2, 1901   October 2, 1982
י״ג בשבט תרס״א   ט״ו בתשרי תשמ״ג

1. Jewish symbols often appear on tombstones. What symbol appears on this monument? _____

2. In what year was the person born? _____

3. In what month did he die? _____

4. How old was he when he died? _____

5. The Hebrew dates of birth and death are often included on a tombstone. This person was born in the Hebrew month of Shevat, which corresponds to the month of February. Can you find the Hebrew word for this month? Write it here: _____

6. In Hebrew, letters can be used in place of numbers. For example, alef=1, bet=2, and so on. Write the Hebrew letters from the tombstone that stand for the Jewish year 5742, which is the same as the year 1982. _____

7. What do the five Hebrew letters at the top of the stone stand for? (See page 85 for a hint.) _____

Conclusion
The Journey Continues

· ·

Nearly four thousand years ago the Jewish people began as one family—the children of Abraham and Sarah. Though we are now spread all over the world, we still feel those strong family ties through the life-cycle rituals and traditions we share.

Whether Jewish babies are born in Alabama or Argentina, they are welcomed into the Jewish community through a *brit* ceremony. Whether Jewish teenagers reach the age of thirteen in Maine or France, they mark the occasion with a Bar Mitzvah or Bat Mitzvah ceremony. Whether Jewish brides and grooms marry in Indiana or Italy, they stand under a wedding *ḥuppah.* Sharing these customs and traditions with other Jewish people helps us know we are members of one large family.

Although our journey through the cycle of life in this book has
ended, for you it has just begun. So much still lies ahead. As you reach
each milestone on your journey, you can celebrate it in a Jewish way.
The words of this blessing express the wonder and thanks we feel as
we achieve each new step:

בָּרוּךְ אַתָּה, ה' אֱלֹהֵינוּ, מֶלֶךְ הָעוֹלָם,
שֶׁהֶחֱיָנוּ וְקִיְּמָנוּ וְהִגִּיעָנוּ לַזְּמַן הַזֶּה.

Praised are You, Adonai our God, who has given us life,
sustained us, and brought us to this season of joy.

GLOSSARY

AHAVAT TZION אַהֲבַת צִיּוֹן
The mitzvah of "Love for Israel."

ALIYAH עֲלִיָּה
The honor of being called up to recite the blessings for the Torah reading.

AUFRUF
Yiddish for "calling up." Refers to the bride and groom's *aliyah* during the Shabbat morning service before the wedding ceremony.

BAL TASH'HIT בַּל תַּשְׁחִית
The mitzvah of "Caring for the Environment."

BAR MITZVAH בַּר מִצְוָה
Hebrew for "Son of the Commandment." The term is used to describe a thirteen-year-old boy who is now responsible for fulfilling God's commandments (mitzvot).

BAT בַּת
Hebrew for "daughter of."

BAT MITZVAH בַּת מִצְוָה
Hebrew for "Daughter of the Commandment." The term is used to describe a twelve-year-old or thirteen-year-old girl who is now responsible for fulfilling God's commandments (mitzvot).

BEN בֶּן
Hebrew for "son of."

BIKKUR HOLIM בִּקּוּר חוֹלִים
The mitzvah of "Visiting the Sick."

BIMAH בִּימָה
The platform in the sanctuary from which the Torah is read.

BRIT בְּרִית
The Covenant, or agreement, between God and the Jewish people.

BRIT BAT בְּרִית בַּת
"Covenant of the Daughter"—the ceremony that welcomes a baby girl into the Jewish people's Covenant with God. Sometimes called Simhat Bat.

BRIT MILAH בְּרִית מִילָה
"Covenant of the Circumcision"—the ceremony which welcomes a baby boy into the Jewish people's covenant with God.

CONFIRMATION
The ceremony that takes place when students are fifteen or sixteen, marking the conclusion of the students' formal religious-school education. The ceremony usually takes place on Shavuot.

CONSECRATE
To make something holy.

CONSECRATION
Literally means "the act of declaring devotion to God." Children take part in a Consecration ceremony, usually on Simhat Torah, when they officially begin their Jewish education.

D'RASH דְּרָשׁ
A short speech about the Torah portion or the haftarah.

D'VAR TORAH דְּבַר תּוֹרָה
A short speech about the Torah portion or the haftarah.

EL MALEI RAHAMIM אֵל מָלֵא רַחֲמִים
The prayer that ends the funeral service and asks God to grant peace and protection to the soul of the person who has died.

EULOGY
A speech at the funeral service which recounts the deceased person's life.

HACHNASAT ORHIM הַכְנָסַת אוֹרְחִים
The mitzvah of "Welcoming Guests."

HAFTARAH הַפְטָרָה
A reading from the prophets that concludes the Torah service.

HATAN חָתָן
Hebrew for "groom."

ḤEVRAH KADDISHA חֶבְרָה קַדִּישָׁא
Jewish burial society.

HIDDUR P'NAI ZAKEN
הִדּוּר פְּנֵי זָקֵן
The mitzvah of "Showing Respect for the Elderly."

ḤUPPAH חֻפָּה
The wedding canopy that a Jewish bride and groom stand under during the marriage ceremony.

JEWISH COMMUNITY
A group of Jewish people who live, work, study, and pray together.

KADDISH קַדִּישׁ
A prayer recited by mourners which praises God's glory and holiness.

KALLAH כַּלָּה
Hebrew for "bride."

KERIAH קְרִיעָה
Hebrew for "tearing." Refers to the act of tearing one's clothing, or cutting a black ribbon that is pinned to one's clothing, as a way of showing the pain we feel when someone we love has died.

KETUBAH כְּתֻבָּה
The marriage contract.

KIBBUD AV VA-EM
כִּבּוּד אָב וָאֵם
The mitzvah of "Honoring Parents."

KIDDUSHIN קִדּוּשִׁין
The Hebrew word for the marriage ceremony, which means "making holy."

K'LAL YISRAEL כְּלַל יִשְׂרָאֵל
Hebrew for "all the people of Israel." Refers to the value that all Jews are responsible for one another, no matter where they live.

MA'ACHIL R'EVIM
מַאֲכִיל רְעֵבִים
The mitzvah of "Feeding the Hungry."

MATZEVAH מַצֵּבָה
Hebrew for "gravestone."

MILAH מִילָה
The Hebrew word for "circumcision."

MINYAN מִנְיָן
The group of ten Jewish adults required for public prayer.

MITZVAH מִצְוָה
A commmandment from God. God's mitzvot teach us how to live a Jewish life.

MITZVOT מִצְוֹת
The Hebrew word for "God's commandments," which teach us how to live a Jewish life.

MOHEL מוֹהֵל
The person who performs the circumcision.

MOURNER
A person whose close relative has recently died.

PIDYON HA-BAT פִּדְיוֹן הַבַּת
"Redeeming the Daughter"— ceremony for a firstborn daughter.

PIDYON HA-BEN פִּדְיוֹן הַבֵּן
"Redeeming the Son"—the ceremony by which a firstborn son is released from the biblical obligation to devote his life to God's service.

RODEF SHALOM רוֹדֵף שָׁלוֹם
The mitzvah of "Pursuing Peace."

SANDEK סַנְדָּק
The person who holds the baby during the circumcision.

SEUDAT HAVRA'AH
סְעוּדַת הַבְרָאָה
Hebrew for "a meal of condolence." Refers to the meal, usually prepared by friends, that is eaten after the mourners return from the cemetery.

SEUDAT MITZVAH סְעוּדַת מִצְוָה
A joyous meal served after the performance of a mitzvah.

SHELOSHIM שְׁלוֹשִׁים
The thirty days of mourning after a funeral.

SHEM TOV שֵׁם טוֹב
Hebrew for "a good name." A person's name becomes a

shem tov when he or she behaves righteously and follows God's commandments.

SHEMIRAH   שְׁמִירָה
The ritual guarding of a body before it is buried.

SHEVAH BRACHOT   שֶׁבַע בְּרָכוֹת
The "Seven Blessings" recited during the marriage ceremony.

SHIVA   שִׁבְעָה
The seven-day mourning period that begins after a funeral.

SH'MIRAT SHABBAT   שְׁמִירַת שַׁבָּת
The mitzvah of "Observing Shabbat."

SHROUD
The burial garment.

SIDDURIM   סִדּוּרִים
(plural of siddur)
Hebrew for "prayerbooks."

SIMḤAH   שִׂמְחָה
Hebrew for "joy." Used to describe a joyous event such as a wedding or the birth of a baby.

SIMḤAT BAT   שִׂמְחַת בַּת
"Rejoicing Over a Daughter"— the ceremony that welcomes a baby girl into the Jewish people's covenant with God. Sometimes called Brit Bat.

SURNAME
A person's last name—the family name.

TAHARAH   טָהֳרָה
The ritual washing of a body in preparation for burial.

TALLIT   טַלִּית
Prayer shawl.

TALMUD TORAH   תַּלְמוּד תּוֹרָה
The mitzvah of "Jewish Learning."

TEFILLAH   תְּפִלָּה
The Hebrew word for "prayer."

TZA'AR BA'ALEI ḤAYYIM
צַעַר בַּעֲלֵי־חַיִּים
The mitzvah of "Having Compassion for Animals."

YAHRZEIT
The anniversary of a person's death.

YIZKOR   יִזְכּוֹר
A prayer service to remember and honor those who have died.